Begun 12-01-04 *finished 12-04-04*

"I JUST WANTED MORE LAND" –JABEZ

A CAREFUL ANALYSIS OF BRUCE WILKINSON'S *THE PRAYER OF JABEZ*

GARY E. GILLEY

xulon PRESS

Susie

"I Just Wanted More Land" –*Jabez*
by Gary E. Gilley

Printed in the United States of America
ISBN 1-931232-55-5

Xulon Press
11350 Random Hills Road
Suite 800
Fairfax, VA 22030
(703) 279-6511
XulonPress.com

DEDICATION

To my faithful wife, Marsha,
the joy and love of my life

CONTENTS

FOREWORD

A few years after Bruce Wilkinson gradu-ated from Dallas Theological Seminary, I entered as a student. I clearly remember sitting in a particular class and the warning that one of our Profs issued to us. He noted that we were receiving the type of education at Dallas Seminary that could be used for good or bad. Our Prof pointed out that we could use our training in the handling of Scripture to expound the meaning of God's Word in its proper context or we could mishandle the text for our own con-nivance and mislead many. He went on to say that those of us who had a lot on the ball could probably start our own successful cult. In the past, I have had a great respect for the ministry of Bruce Wilkinson and Walk Thru the Bible Ministries. I am now concerned that Dr. Wilkinson has used his gifts and training to start a "Prayer of Jabez" cult.

Why do I think this? In short, because Bruce Wilkinson's wildly popular *The Prayer of Jabez* has become Exhibit A for Scripture twisting in recent times. Nowhere in Dr. Wilkinson's little book does he take the time to set the passage of 1 Chronicles 4:9-10 in its historical context, which both he and I were trained to do at Dallas Seminary in the 1970s. Why is this important? I am reminded of a little saying that should help. It says, "Scripture taken out of context is a pretext." Pretext means an "alleged reason," or "ploy." That is exactly what Dr. Wilkinson's *The Prayer of Jabez* is when compared to how God chose to present these two verses in the context of 1 Chronicles 4.

Instead of explaining the meaning of this passage in its original context, Dr. Wilkinson chose to explain it in relation to what he wanted it to mean. Instead of setting the passage in the historical context of the argument of Chronicles, Dr. Wilkinson set it into the context of his own personal life, as a success for life mantra that has in essence brought him good luck throughout most of his adult life. Instead of explaining textual factors from the passage itself so that those verses would be controlled by the context, Dr. Wilkinson repackages Jabez' prayer with infomercial-like testimonies about how it has worked in his own life and the lives of many others with which he has shared its "meaning."

Since 1 Chronicles 4:9-10 does not teach what Dr. Wilkinson suggests, in spite of the impressive number of evangelical superstars who arise to support this erroneous presentation, it requires a presentation, such as his book, in order to sell his idea. In like manner, it requires another presentation to rebut the error of Dr. Wilkinson and clarify a proper approach and understanding. This service has been rendered to the evangelical community by Pastor Gary Gilley. Pastor Gilley respectfully notes many of the errors in Dr. Wilkinson's little book and then provides a proper interpretation of the passage. He does this by examining 1 Chronicles 4:9-10 in its original context, the way that Dr. Wilkinson and I were taught years ago at Dallas Seminary. Pastor Gilley does not stop with an exposition of the prayer of Jabez, but also provides a much-needed reminder to his readers of the general principles that one should use when approaching God's inerrant Word.

As Pastor Gilley reminds us, it is the responsibility of Christian leaders to point out error, especially a pastor to his flock (Titus 1:9; 2

Timothy 4:2-4). This book provides a timely, much needed, well-thought out, and biblically sound response to the prayer of Jabez cult that has been developed by Dr. Wilkinson's little book. I highly recommend *I Just Wanted More Land–Jabez* for anyone wanting to properly understand this scriptural passage.

Dr. Thomas Ice
Executive Director,
The Pre-Trib Research Center

PREFACE

Today's greatest theological war is being fought over the Bible, and the battle rages on many fronts. Those reading this little volume, as well as Bruce Wilkinson's *The Prayer of Jabez*, are hopefully not among those who deny Scripture. To them, that battle has been won, and the Word of God reigns supreme as the final, inspired authority over all faith and practice. Such believers stand on guard at the gate of the Christian faith, refusing entry to all who would directly attack the veracity of the Bible. This we applaud and happily stand at the ready with them. But sadly, while the front gate is amply defended, someone has left the back gate wide open—and few seem to notice. Flowing through this undefended gate are hoards of issues, theories, approaches, distortions, and sloppy interpretations that undermine the Scriptures as effectively as those who would deny its authority.

It is this back gate that concerns us. Bruce Wilkinson would undoubtedly stand shoulder to shoulder with all true lovers of the Word of God. Indeed, he would most likely give his life in its defense. But at the same time, he is leading a charge through the back gate that is popularizing a lethal approach to Scripture. His book, which is surely well meaning, is doing incalculable damage within the walls of the conservative church.

I have written this book in an effort to stem this tide of unbiblical teaching emanating from *The Prayer of Jabez.* But the issue is wider than that; the real concern is how do we approach, interpret, and apply Scripture. It is here, more than in anything else, that Wilkinson has done a great disservice to God's people. As a result, I have decided to present my case in both positive and negative ways. First, negatively, I will dismantle not only Wilkinson's interpretations of Scripture, but also his whole approach to the precious Word of God. And then, having torn down his system, I have presented a positive framework for understanding the Bible. Thus, in Part Two, I will offer a short guide on how to study the Bible. I trust that this two-pronged approach will both warn and edify.

SECTION ONE

THE JABEZ PRAYER— AN ANALYSIS

Introduction

In 1975, Bruce Wilkinson made his first attempt to publish a book concerning the prayer of Jabez, but to no avail. Apparently few were interested in an obscure little prayer by an obscure man hidden away in an obscure section of the Old Testament. After all, what did anyone know about Jabez, or his prayer for that matter? And since little was known about either, most figured there could not be much profit in reading a whole book on the subject. At least that seemed to be the reasoning 26 years ago. My, how things have changed. For some mysterious reason, Jabez has caught on. In every nook and cranny of the conservative church, one hears discussion and testimony about the **Jabez prayer**, the **Jabez blessing**, the **Jabez miracles**, etc. Focus on the Family recently declared the Jabez prayer to be the greatest thing to happen to Christianity in twenty years. It is for these reasons that I have taken the time to evaluate and challenge this extremely popular book. Although I take no pleasure in "picking a fight" with a fellow Christian, I sincerely believe that the prayer of Jabez, as Wilkinson explains it, is a false teaching that is deceiving many and must be exposed (Titus 1:9). This I will endeavor to do in the following pages, with love and humility, recognizing that Wilkinson most likely has the best of intentions. Nevertheless, what he teaches in his small book is not what the Bible teaches, and that is ultimately what matters.

Before we actually examine what Dr. Wilkinson has written, it might be wise to consider why a book that could not get off the ground in 1975 is a runaway best seller in the twenty-first century. What has changed to bring about such a difference? Scriptures certainly have not changed. What Wilkinson was teaching in 1975 was a mistake then, and it is a mistake now; I will clearly demonstrate this in a few moments. No, the Scriptures have not changed, but the way many believers approach Scripture, their hermeneutics, has changed.

Hermeneutics! Now I ask you, is that any way to catch the attention of readers? Experts say we must grab the reader's interest in the early stages of a writing or chance losing our audience altogether. Yet I must take that risk, for if there is a cancer eating out the heart of conservative Christianity, it is largely hermeneutical in nature. Why is it, some ask, that so many fine Christians come up with different interpretations of Scripture and of the Christian life? The blame can often be laid at the doorstep of hermeneutics. Why is it that some, like me, are strongly opposed to such a well-received book as *The Prayer of Jabez*? Again, we can point a finger at hermeneutics.

Hermeneutics is the science, and perhaps art, that teaches the principles, laws, and methods of interpretation. Anyone reading anything has a hermeneutical approach to what he or she reads. We interpret what we read in the light of principles that govern our understanding of the material. Whether it is the newspaper, tax forms, a legal document, or a novel, we can truly understand what we read only when we are using the proper hermeneutic.

When it comes to most literature, the method of interpretation that must be applied, if the material is to be understood as intended, is called "normal" or "literal" hermeneutics. That is, the information is to be understood literally, as are most things in life. There may be figures of speech, metaphors, and the like, but those are all recognized as part of normal language and interpreted accordingly.

When it comes to Scripture, unfortunately, a number of other hermeneutical approaches have been developed in a misguided attempt to understand the "real" meaning of a biblical text. This is the path that Bruce Wilkinson is traveling in *The Prayer of Jabez*. He does not interpret the prayer in a normal manner; rather, he devotionalizes or spiritualizes the text, inventing meanings never intended by the biblical author. Then on the basis of this faulty understanding of the passage, he develops applications that he believes are universal in nature. As we carefully examine *The Prayer of Jabez*, these errors, and the dangers they represent, will become obvious.

D.A. Carson, writing on a completely different subject (suffering), is on the mark when he proclaims:

> One of the major causes of devastating grief and confusion among Christians is that our expectations are false.... If ...our beliefs are largely out of step with God who has disclosed himself in the Bible and supremely in Jesus, then the pain from the personal tragedy may be multiplied many

times over as we begin to question the very foundations of our faith (*How Long O Lord*, p. 9).

What is true in the face of pain is true in the everyday life of the Christian. If our belief system is out of step with the truth of God, if our expectations are not in line with Scripture, then our disappointments, when encountered by reality, will be greatly intensified. Wilkinson has painted a false picture of God, prayer, and the Christian life in general. The fallout as millions of his followers discover this will be ugly at best. Hopefully this little volume will help many to avoid the inevitable head-on collision when truth meets the fantasies perpetrated by *The Prayer of Jabez*.

CHAPTER ONE

THE BIG PICTURE

One of His disciples said to Him, "Lord, teach us to pray" (Luke 11:1). And Jesus said to them, "Have you boys heard of the prayer of Jabez? It is a little prayer hidden away in Chronicles that will absolutely revolutionize your prayer life. As a matter of fact, it is a prayer which, if you pray it on a regular basis, is guaranteed to unlock the power of God in your life. I, Myself, have been praying this prayer since I was twelve years old, and continue to pray it every day."

To hear all the praise being poured out on Bruce Wilkinson's book, *The Prayer of Jabez,* the unaware child of God might swear that this was surely Jesus' response, but of course it was not. As a matter of fact, neither Jabez, nor his prayer, is mentioned beyond the scope of I Chronicles 4. David did not write a psalm about it, Jesus did not mention it, and the epistles, while calling on us to pray without ceasing, are silent on the subject. Paul, in his marvelous New Testament prayers (e.g., Ephesians 1:15-23; 3:14-21; Colossians 1:9-14) ignores it. At no time or place in all of the Word of God are we commanded, told to examine, follow as a model, or repeat daily the prayer of Jabez. So why all the excitement? Why has this simple 92-page book become the best-selling book in the Christian community and one of the most popular in the country? (The official web site, *prayerofjabez.com*, reports that six million copies have been sold in the first year alone, and that it is the fastest selling book in the country.) Why is it being promoted in every corner of Christianity? It is as if the key to the Christian life has suddenly been unearthed in some Palestinian cave. If you question the accuracy of my comments, just examine some of the published testimonies praising this prayer.

> Do you want to be extravagantly blessed by God? Are you ready to reach for the extraordinary? To ask God for the abundant blessings He longs to give you? Join

Bruce Wilkinson to discover how the remarkable prayer of a little-known Bible hero can release God's favor, power, and protection. You'll see how one daily prayer can help you leave the past behind—and break through to the life you were meant to live. (Back cover of the book.)

Howard Hendricks says, "If you long to live your life the way it is meant to be lived in Christ, *The Prayer of Jabez* is a must read. A small book, a life-changing message! Highly recommended!" (Back cover of the book.)

Unleash the supernatural power of God in your life! In his best-selling book *The Prayer of Jabez*, Dr. Bruce Wilkinson, president of Walk Thru the Bible Ministries, shows you how a simple daily prayer can enable you to experience the blessings God longs to lavish upon us.... Learn how to experience His miraculous power and blessing for yourself by praying this audacious, four-part prayer. (Christian Book Distributor advertisement.)

A recent search on Yahoo! brought up 2,410

matches on the "Prayer of Jabez." I ran through the first 200 sites and found nothing but praise for this prayer. The majority of the sites were either selling Jabez-related products (through an already established industry selling everything from Jabez T-shirts to hats to videos and cassettes) or publishing testimonies of changed lives contributed to praying the Jabez prayer.

For some inexplicable reason, this newest fad is flying under the radar of even otherwise discerning Christians. Had Bruce Wilkinson published a book encouraging the people of God to pray, asking God to expand their ministries for Him, we would cheer. If such a volume were securely grounded in biblical principles of prayer, who could complain? But had Wilkinson written such a book, it would also have been largely ignored in the Christian community. Today's Christians seem to need a gimmick to catch their attention. Hype and anecdotal testimony motivate them, for in this way many have been trained to discern truth from error. If it carries the label "Christian," and if it appears to work, it is automatically assumed to be God's truth. And what an exciting concept: The discovery of a relatively unknown prayer, promising to be the key to unlock the door to the blessings of God. Who could imagine that this simple prayer, which needs only to be repeated verbatim on a regular basis, would hold the secret to so much power and abundance? And who could imagine so many Christians falling for such an idea?

At its best, Wilkinson's study of the prayer of Jabez is poor, as we will see. ***But first we must expose the major error behind his teaching— that the repetition of a prayer, any prayer, even a biblical prayer, unlocks the power of God in our lives.*** This is the claim and appeal of the book, and it is clearly unbiblical.

REPETITIVE PRAYER

In a local paper, an ad is placed weekly that reads, "St. Jude Novena: May the Sacred Heart of Jesus be adored, glorified, loved and preserved throughout the world now & forever. Sacred Heart of Jesus, pray for us. St. Jude, Worker of Miracles, pray for us. St. Jude, Helper of the Hopeless, pray for us. Amen. Say this prayer 9 times each day for 9 Days, then publish and your prayers will be answered. It has never been known to fail. Thank you, St. Jude." This prayer, used by some Catholics, was the first thing that came to my mind upon reading *The Prayer of Jabez*. In fact, the opening words of the book, still in the preface are, "I want to teach you how to pray a daring prayer that God always answers.... In fact, thousands of believers who are applying its truths are seeing miracles happen on a regular basis." This promise of miracles, by the way, is a major emphasis of the book, being repeated often throughout (pp. 24, 25, 43, 44, 56, 58, 68, 77, 82, 90, 92).

The prayer itself is very simple. Buried in the seldom-read genealogical section of I Chronicles, the whole account is found in two verses (4:9,10*):*

> **And Jabez was more honorable than his brothers, and his mother named him Jabez, saying, "Because I bore him with pain." Now Jabez called on the God of Israel, saying, "Oh that Thou wouldst bless me indeed, and enlarge my border, and that Thy hand might be with me, and that Thou wouldst keep me from harm, that it may not pain me!" And God granted him what he requested (NKJV).**

The details of this prayer, and how Wilkinson explains and applies them, will be examined later, but for now our attention must be focused on how he suggests this prayer should be used in general.

VAIN REPETITION

Wilkinson apparently recommends the use of this prayer in two ways. First, it is to be repeated word for word. For thirty years the author has been praying the prayer in this manner (p. 11). He assures us that if we will do the same, the Jabez prayer will have significant impact on our lives. How can he be so certain? Does he base his promise on the revelation of God? Can it be found in the biblical examples of godly men and women? Is it grounded in scriptural precept and command? Not at all, but rather his experiences are Wilkinson's foundation for truth: "How do I know it will significantly impact you? Because of my experience and the testimony of hundreds of others around the world with whom I've shared these principles" (p. 11). "Story-theology," as I like to label it, is the footing for this new teaching. Warning bells and whistles should be going off in the minds and hearts of every discerning believer at this point. Our faith is not founded on story-theology, testimonies, or the abstruse experiences of men and women. It is rooted totally in Scripture. Scripture nowhere promises what Wilkinson does. Wilkinson cannot, nor does he attempt to, support his numerous ideas and applications found in *The Prayer of Jabez* by the Scriptures (except through his extremely poor exegesis of the passage itself). He must by necessity resort to experiences and testimonies. Surely none of us have to be reminded that everything—from diet plans to snake oil to Christian Science to Hindu mysticism—is promoted by testimony and anecdotal evidence. Such testimony proves nothing. Only appeal to the Word confirms truth.

At this point a serious question must be addressed: Do the Scriptures call for repetitive prayers? Are we ever instructed to repeat someone else's prayer as our own? And if so, are we promised a great blessing? Some have tried to find a biblical base for repetitive prayer. In a recent *Christianity Today* article, Arthur Paul Boers attempted to lend some kind of biblical support for the recent resurgence in repetitive prayers, spiritual pilgrimages to monasteries, and interest in the pre-Reformation liturgy and forms of worship which many call the *daily office*. He documents that interest in such forms can be found in the early church, which itself borrowed from Jewish tradition:

The early church encouraged morning and evening prayer (which included the Lord's Prayer and praying the Psalms). The Didache (perhaps as early as A.D. 60) dictated that the Lord's Prayer be said three times a day, in imitation of Jewish prayers (*Christianity Today*, Jan. 8, 2001, "Learning the Ancient Rhythms of Prayer" by Arthur Paul Boers, p. 40).

Boers reinforces his emphasis on repetitive prayers by quoting from David Adam's book, *The Rhythm of Life*, "That is true of most people: if they're left without an office, without prayers they learn and recite, they tend to pray very little" (ibid. p. 41). These men succeed in showing the early roots of repetitive prayers, both Jewish and Christian. Some in the Jewish and Christian circles chanted repetitive phrases as a part of worship; however, there is absolutely no evidence that this was a widespread practice until the church was Romanized years later. But most importantly, what these authors failed to do was to show that such practices have a biblical basis. When Jesus came, He smashed many of the rituals of the Jews. He condemned the Pharisees for invalidating the Word of God by their traditions, and He clearly warned that they had allowed their culture, customs and ceremonies to supersede and override the Word of God (Matthew 15:6). Rather than duplicating the mistakes of the past, we should learn from them, and then move on to a biblically supported view of prayer.

Jesus' words are much clearer: *"And when you are praying, do not use meaningless repetition, as the Gentiles do, for they suppose that they will be heard for their many words"* (Matthew 6:8). Following this statement Jesus immediately gave His disciples a model prayer, one that we usually call "The Lord's Prayer." But there is absolutely no indication that our Savior ever intended even this archetype to be a prayer of repetition. We never, for instance, find Jesus leading His disciples in a recitation of this prayer. Nor do we find any mention of it in the New Testament church, the book of Acts, or the epistles. It clearly was never intended to be a prayer to be repeated verbatim; it was simply a model prayer, an example. The disciples asked Jesus to teach them how to pray, not to give them a prayer (Luke 11:1), and that is exactly what He did.

In some ways Wilkinson's error is more destructive than that of the pre-Reformation church. As confused and misguided as many of the early believers may have been, their goal seemed to be to grow in their knowledge and honor of God. They were seeking the elusive "holy life" in unbiblical ways. What Wilkinson suggests is not a means by which we can become more holy (holiness in not on the table in this book), but a **formula** by which we can get what we want from God. Wilkinson says of Jabez's last request (which we will examine in more detail in a moment), "[It] is a brilliant but little-understood **strategy** for sustaining a blessed life" (p. 63) (emphasis added). Later Wilkinson issues this challenge, "Make the Jabez prayer for blessing part of the daily fabric of your life. To do that, I encourage you to follow unwaveringly the plan outlined here for the next thirty days. By the end of that time, you'll be noticing significant changes in your life, and the prayer will be on its way to becoming a treasured, lifelong habit" (p. 86). The Jabez prayer, as Wilkinson suggests using it, is not a means by which we grow in godliness (which also would be a misuse of the prayer); it is a gimmick by which we can tap God for His storehouse of blessings.

Some, having already been indoctrinated by the message of this book, will protest at this point. They will say that the Jabez prayer is to be used for expanding our ministries. And while Wilkinson recommends using the prayer for this purpose, note how Wilkinson himself suggests it also be used and how his readers understand him. First, Wilkinson gives this example:

> If Jabez had worked on Wall Street, he might have prayed, "Lord, increase the value of my investment portfolios." When I talk to presidents of companies, I often talk to them about this particular mind-set. When Christian executives ask me, "Is it right for me to ask God for more business?" my response is, "Absolutely!" If you're doing your business God's way, it's not only right to ask for more, but He is waiting for you to ask. Your business is the territory God has entrusted to you. He wants you to accept it as a significant opportunity to touch individual lives, the business community, and the larger world for His glory. Asking Him to enlarge that opportunity brings Him only delight (pp. 31, 32).

How sad that the saints recorded in Hebrews 11:36-38 had not heard of the power of the Jabez prayer. Perhaps they could have avoided the beatings, agonizing deaths, destitute lives, homelessness, and pain they suffered for the sake of Christ. God did not increase the boundaries of these believers. He reduced them. Were they out of God's will, or had they just never heard of the prayer that "guarantees to release the blessings of God"?

Wilkinson's message is not unclear to his audience. Following are two testimonies pulled from his Web site (*prayerofjabez.com*) that clearly demonstrate how his readers understand the message of the book:

> God has spoken to me unmistakably in several different ways. I've woken up at 3 A.M. remembering vividly detailed dreams—as I lay there, I knew perfectly what He was telling me. I've found books, pamphlets, letters and even cards I hadn't seen in years, at times when I'm looking for a pencil or something, that are exactly what I need [*sic*] at the time.
>
> I wanted to share the blessing that I got when I prayed this prayer. I had been given the book and was told of testimonies from reading this book and praying this prayer. I had three divine appointments. Each time this prayer was mentioned, I gave the book back to its

owner and promised to buy my own copy. Well, I finally did.... I was struggling with my business—I am a hairdresser, and I love doing hair, but I was not making enough money to meet our needs at home. I prayed the Jabez prayer and got three phone calls from clients, praise God!!!

Such testimonies are enough to get me to pray the Jabez prayer (almost). I have lost hundreds of pens and a handful of reading glasses, not to mention untold wealth in the form of change that has fallen from my pockets down the side of the couch. If I begin to pray this prayer, who knows what I might recover? And with each stock market slide, I suggest that some Jabez supporters call a "National Day of Jabez Praying" for the enlargement of our financial borders. After all, the Lord's work will certainly suffer if American Christians go broke.

THE APPLICATION

The second way that Wilkinson apparently recommends using Jabez's prayer is to pray for ourselves, assisted by his four-step example. Verbatim repetition of the Jabez prayer is where the novice begins, but it quickly leads to using the prayer as a model for our own prayer life. Although God never encourages us to pattern our prayer life after Jabez, Wilkinson assures us that we should. And although Wilkinson takes great liberties with his interpretation of Jabez's prayer, forcing it to say far more than it does (as we will see), he obviously believes that we can glean from this one prayer everything we need for a blessed life. This is, of course, the appeal of the book: pray a simple prayer, use it as a paradigm for your own prayer life, and presto-chango, guaranteed blessings galore. The following are some representative statements taken from the book:

> The Jabez prayer **distills** God's powerful will for your future (pp. 11, 12).

> I want to show you just how dramatically each of Jabez's requests can **release** something **miraculous** in your life (p. 15).
> When was the last time you saw **miracles** happen on a regular basis in your life? (p. 17).

> A **guaranteed by-product** of praying the Jabez prayer: "Your life will become

marked by **miracles**. How do I know? Because He promises it, and I've seen it happen in my own!" (p. 24).

Through a simple, believing prayer, **you can change** your future. You can change what happens one minute from now (p. 29).

You will be like John and Peter, who were given words to say at the moment they needed them (pp. 41–42).

We can have a front-row seat in a life of **miracles** (pp. 43–44).

Seeking God's blessings [in our lives] is our ultimate act of worship (p. 49).

You and I are always only **one plea away from inexplicable**, Spirit-enabled exploits. By His touch you can experience supernatural enthusiasm, boldness and power. It is up to you (pp. 60–61).

As you repeat the steps you will **set in motion** a cycle of blessings (p. 83).

It's only what you believe will happen and therefore do next that will **release** God's power for you (p. 87).

God will **release** His **miraculous** power in your life now (p. 92).

(Emphasis added throughout quotes.)

THE APPEAL OF JABEZ

Jabez and his prayer are popular with the Christian masses for at least two reasons. First, there is nothing that people love better than a quick-fix "wonder cure" for whatever ails them. Signs posted all over our city read, "Lose 30 pounds in 30 days." Pills are advertised on television that promise to absorb so much fat that we will be able to eat anything we want and still lose weight. Weekend seminars pledge to heal broken marriages. And some guy, who has gone bankrupt twice, promises to teach us how to become millionaires buying real estate, all for just a few hours of our time and only $495. Wilkinson has caught this wave. We want spirituality and blessings from God, and we want them in a hurry. Who has time for true Bible study, in-depth fellowship, and intimate prayer?

But if we could be given a secret formula containing a short, simple prayer guaranteed to revolutionize our lives, how sweet it would be.

Wilkinson's book also succeeds because of what it guarantees. As can be seen from the quotes above, the author promises that a simple prayer has the ability to release (*distill*) the power and miracles of God into our lives. But Jabez's prayer does no such thing. Wilkinson has taken a prayer of a seemingly godly man, ripped it out of context, misinterpreted most of it, and inappropriately applied it to his and others' lives. And, inexplicably, many Christians have been duped.

CHAPTER TWO

DETAILS, DETAILS

"Is it possible that God wants you to be self-ish in your prayer? To ask for more—and more again—from your Lord?… I want to show you that such a prayer is not the self-centered act it might appear, but a supremely spiritual one and exactly the kind of request our Father longs to hear" (p. 19). Statements like these have piqued the interest of millions of readers of Bruce Wilkinson's wildly popular book. In the previous chapter, we attempted to outline two fundamental flaws in the Jabez prayer, as being used by Wilkinson. The first such flaw is the incredible idea that the verbatim repetition of an Old Testament prayer, or any prayer for that matter, unlocks "God's favor, power, and protection," as the back cover of the book promises. The second flaw is the idea that the prayer of Jabez is meant to be a model prayer—one that we follow in our own prayer life with miraculous results. Our first chapter looked at the big picture; in this one we will examine the details. We will find that not only is Wilkinson completely off base in his overall use of the Jabez prayer, but he has also sadly misinterpreted and misapplied the prayer itself.

Before we go any further, I know that someone will be complaining, "How can you 'attack' a man and a work that has done so much good for so many people?" Our answer is that we are not attempting to attack a man, but we are trying to defend the faith (Jude 3) and to protect the flock of God from those who would "introduce destructive heresies" (Acts 20:28-32). Wilkinson's teachings concerning Jabez's prayer are seriously in error and must be exposed and refuted (Titus 1:9).

A PROPER UNDERSTANDING OF THE PRAYER OF JABEZ

Jabez began his life in pain (apparently for his mother), but eventually became an honorable man (I Chronicles 4:9). At some point in his life, he uttered a prayer that God saw fit to record. The prayer of Jabez comes in four parts, Wilkinson tells us (actually it comes in five parts, but for some reason Wilkinson does not quote the last line, which reads, "That I may not cause pain"—NKJV):

Oh, that You would bless me indeed,
and enlarge my territory,
that Your hand would be with me,
and that You would keep me from evil.
(I Chronicles 4:10, NKJV).

The prayer is followed with the phrase, "And God granted him what he requested." The proper exegesis of this passage would be to recognize that Jabez, being an honorable man (at least he was more honorable than his brothers— I Chronicles 4:9), sincerely cried out to God for something that was on his heart and mind. God graciously answered that prayer, for He delights in answering the prayers of a righteous man (James 5:16). We should follow the pattern of this decent man and lift our concerns to the Lord (Philippians 4:6). Jabez might then be used as an example of a man of prayer. That is about as far as we can go, in all honesty. Anything beyond this is pure speculation, or worse, the allegorizing of Scripture. (See chapter four for the danger of this approach to Scripture.)

Looking closer, we find that Jabez's prayer was answered, but we don't know what he specifically desired, except it had something to do with enlarging his territory. Again, we are unclear about Jabez's particular concern. Was he having boundary disputes? Was he at war with the heathen nations around him, or perhaps with his dishonorable brothers? Had someone stolen some of his land? We do not know, but we do know that a literal understanding of this passage would have something to do with physical land, not spiritual ministries. *"That you would keep me from evil"* (NKJV) is translated in the NASB as *"That Thou wouldst keep me from harm."* The final phrase is rendered in the NASB as *"That it may not pain me."* It would appear that, far from a prayer to increase his ministry, Jabez was praying for protection. He seemed to be faced with a potentially dangerous and harmful situation from which he needed safety. Our best guess is that he desired to resolve border disputes with his enemies. He prayed for protection and an enlargement of his territory, and God answered his prayers. In addition, we do not hear of him praying this prayer at any other time in his life. Rather than repeating the same words over and over for thirty years, he very well may have prayed these words only once. There is no indication that Jabez saw his prayer as a means of "releasing the power of God" for ministry, financial success, finding lost pencils, or miracles. Our best understanding of the text would be that he was facing a seriously dangerous and harmful situation, and he believed he needed the protective hand of God. He prayed for that protection, and God answered his prayer. End of story. Now let's see how Wilkinson interprets and applies the same text. We will study each phrase separately.

Oh, that You would bless me indeed!

It is interesting that, out of the literally hundreds of prayers in Scripture that Wilkinson could have chosen, he selected the only one in which an individual specifically asked for God to bless him. The phrase "bless me" is found only seven times in the Bible. Four of those occasions are found in the shameful account of Jacob robbing Esau of his blessing (Genesis 27:19-38). A fifth time was by Pharaoh as he pleaded with Moses to bless him at the Exodus (Exodus 12:32). The final time, apart from Jabez, is when Jacob wrestled with the angel (who may have been the preincarnate Christ), which could hardly be considered prayer in the normal sense, because it is uncertain if Jacob even knew who this being was (Genesis 32:26). If we broaden our research further, we find that of the nearly 500 uses of the words "bless" (including "blessed," "blessing" or "blessings"), we learn much. What we discover is that the principal use of this word group is in the context of three things: 1) blessing or praising God (Judges 5:9; Psalms 16:7, 103:2); 2) pronouncing blessings on people (Ruth 2:4); and 3) declaring those who meet certain conditions blessed (Deuteronomy 30:16, Psalm 5:12). On a few occasions, the Lord is asked directly to bless the nation of Israel (Deuteronomy 26:15; Psalm 67:1). And David asked God to bless his house forever (II Samuel 7:29), a reference to the covenant that God had already made with David (7:16). In addition, church age saints would be wise to ponder two facts. That they have already been "blessed with every spiritual blessing" (Ephesians 1:3). Secondly, not only is there no request in the New Testament epistles for God to bless us, but every mention of God doing so is in reference to spiritual blessings, not material (e.g. Romans 4:6; Galatians 3:14).

The point is this: While God often promises to bless those who meet certain conditions, nowhere else in Scripture do we find an individual directly asking God to bless him. Wilkinson has taken an obscure prayer, applied a questionable meaning to it, and pressed it into service as the perfect example of the way God wants us to pray. If this is how God wants the believer to pray, then why did He not often and clearly teach this model throughout the Scriptures? Why would He insert this marvelous instruction in the genealogical section of the Old Testament, and then dare us to find it? Why would He not give us other examples, direct commands, and detailed methodologies on how to ask God for blessings? This is, of course, not to say that God does not want to hear our petitions. He wants us to bring before Him the concerns of our hearts, and even to pray for our daily bread (Matthew 6:11). But the centerpiece of prayer is not to be, as Wilkinson teaches, the plea for God to "bless me."

Obviously, this prayer is chosen because it is the type of prayer that relates well to our current generation of Christians. It is a selfish prayer, our author assures us (p. 19), yet it is also "a supremely spiritual one and exactly the kind of request our Father longs to hear" (p. 19). If this is true, why didn't our Father tell us so? It is worth observing that Wilkinson supports his theory with a hypothetical illustration of a godly man who prays selfishly (pp. 18, 19). He does not defend his position by the use of biblical examples and other Scriptures, for he cannot. His whole theory lives and dies on Jabez hill. If I can pray selfishly, receive blessings from God, and be spiritual, all at the same time, what a deal! What we have here is the sanctification of selfishness, and of course this is one of the attractions of *The Prayer of Jabez.*

A contrast with the words of Jesus could not be more startling. Our Lord declared that it is the poor in spirit who are blessed. It is those who mourn, are gentle, hunger and thirst for righteousness, are merciful, are pure in heart, are peacemakers, and are persecuted for the sake of righteousness who are blessed of God (Matthew 5:3-11). Such concepts are conspicuously absent from *The Prayer of Jabez.*

To further bolster his case, Wilkinson assures us that when we pray this way, our "life will become marked by miracles. How do I know? He promises it, and I've seen it happen in my own" (pp. 24, 25). I know of no place in Scripture, including I Chronicles 4, where we are **promised** miracles because of prayer. Again, Wilkinson can offer no biblical backing, so he hurries to offer his personal testimony. Later in the same chapter, we learn that "God's bounty is limited only by us, not by His resources, power, or willingness to give. Jabez was blessed simply because he refused to let any obstacle, person, or opinion loom larger than God's nature. And God's nature is to bless.... Through a simple, believing prayer, you can change your future. You can change what happens one minute from now" (p. 29). The above quote is a sad example of half-truths, conjecture, hype, and a demonstration of how far the author is willing to bend to try to prove his point. Wilkinson's theology is much closer to the prosperity gospel than to biblical Christianity, even though he denies it (p. 24). In the prosperity gospel, miracles are constantly being promised when we meet certain conditions. The proof that God will deliver is always based on testimonials, not on the foundation of Scripture. Wilkinson has borrowed a page from the prosperity gospel's handbook and is offering it to Christians, some of whom perhaps have never been exposed to such teaching before. And he is doing so with great success.

Oh, that You would enlarge my territory!

In its simplest form, Wilkinson's challenge is

on target. When he says we should pray, "O God and King, please expand my opportunities and my impact in such a way that I touch more lives for Your glory. Let me do more for you" (p. 32), he is on the money. Far too many Christians are content with doing very little, or nothing at all, for His glory. Wilkinson is right to challenge the children of God to reach out with boldness, enthusiasm, and in the power of the Holy Spirit. Wilkinson is wrong, however, in using the prayer of Jabez to issue this challenge.

The best that I can figure is that Wilkinson has a message to spread, and he is using the prayer of Jabez as his platform. Every first year Bible school student knows the difference between exegesis and eisegesis, and Dr. Wilkinson does too, which should give us reason to contemplate why he chose to ignore the principles of hermeneutics that he knows very well. Exegesis is discovering the meaning of a given text of Scripture. Eisegesis is bringing to a text one's own ideas, bias, or the like, rather than unearthing the meaning of the text itself. Wilkinson does not exegete this passage; he brings to it an idea and forces the text to say what he desires. Along the way he twists and turns almost every word to suit his purpose. Let's take a look.

Wilkinson launches into this portion of Jabez's prayer with this statement: "From both the context and the result of Jabez's prayer, we can see that there was more to his request than a simple desire for more real estate. He wanted more influence, more responsibility, and more opportunity to make a mark for the God of Israel" (p. 30). **This is simply not true**. We know absolutely nothing of Jabez's desire to make a greater impact for the God of Israel. All we know is that he wanted more land, period! For reasons that are not given, God chooses to answer this prayer. This is the exegesis. A proper application might be that we should make our requests known to the God who answers prayer. Rather than doing this, the author decides to use his imagination and force on the text, on Jabez, and on the reader the message he wants to deliver—not the message God revealed in this passage of Scripture.

Having done that, Wilkinson next moves to the application, which takes up the rest of the chapter. Keep in mind, at this point, that Wilkinson has conjured up his own meaning, based upon his misuse of the biblical text. It is upon this eisegesis that he now develops his applications. I trust that the danger and folly of this example of Bible study can be plainly seen.

This is the methodology used by so many to prove anything from the Bible. It is the wrong-minded hermeneutic that is common in too many Christian circles that has done so much damage to believers. *The Prayer of Jabez* is just the most recent example.

In the way of application, Wilkinson delivers a number of anecdotal, superficial, and unsubstantiated illustrations to strengthen his case. He then writes, "Our God specialized in working through normal people who believe in a super-normal God who will do His work through them" (p. 41). We would agree with this statement. A problem develops, however, when he puts this philosophy into working order. When it comes to ministry, Wilkinson informs us that our abilities, experience, and training are of little value (p. 40). What is needed is our willingness and weakness coupled with God's will and power (p. 41). This is an oversimplification and an unbiblical view of ministry. Surely all depends on the power of God, but the New Testament picture is that God uniquely equips and gifts believers for a ministry in the Body of Christ (I Corinthians 12). Not every believer is capable of every ministry even though Wilkinson promises that God "will never send someone to [us] whom [we] cannot help by His leading and strength" (p. 41). Neither does the Bible dismiss our need for training. God wants us to be trained in the understanding of Scripture (II Timothy 2:2,14,15; 3:15-4:5; Hebrews 5:11-14). This kind of training is not emphasized by Wilkinson because he believes that we will "be like John and Peter, who were given the words to say at the moment they needed them" (pp. 41-42). But Jesus did not even promise this to John and Peter in relationship to ministry. The context of Luke 12:11,12 (which Wilkinson fails to mention) has to do with saints standing before authorities as they are being persecuted, and that apparently during the Tribulation (cp. Luke 21:15). By contrast, I Peter 3:15 commands believers today to always be "ready to make a defense to everyone who asks you to give an account for the hope that is in you." This "let go and let God" brand of the Christian faith has been around for a long time, but it certainly fails the test of Scripture.

To solidify his case, Wilkinson promises that those who ask for an enlarged territory will have a "front-row seat in a life of miracles" (p. 43). No less than eight times in the final two pages of this chapter, "miracles" are mentioned. The author tells us that Jabez needed one (we don't know this); that praying this section of the Jabez prayer "releases miracles" (p. 44) (a pure fabrication); and "at that moment, heaven sends angels, resources, strength, and the people you need" (p. 44). How does he know this? We would agree that our God is sufficient for our every need, but He does not promise to bless our every effort for Him with visible success. Wilkinson may have "seen it happen hundreds of times," but tens of thousands of God's godly servants all over the world labor faithfully with little or no measurable results. Are we to conclude, as Wilkinson implies, that the one thing needed for incredible success and miracles is for these poor folks to learn the Jabez prayer? Is God's power really waiting for these men and women of God to stumble upon the right formula before it can be released? Surely few are that naïve.

Oh, that Your hand would be with me!

Wilkinson appears to be an extremely careless student of Scripture. This is perhaps the simplest line in the Jabez prayer, and yet this seminary-trained, world-renowned Bible teacher missteps at virtually every turn. Starting with the positive, Wilkinson tells us, "The 'hand of the Lord' is a biblical term for God's power and presence in the lives of His people" (p. 54). If so, and if we can buy this definition, Jabez was asking for God's power and presence in His life, at least concerning the border issue that was at the core of his prayer. Once again, this is as far as we can honestly take the meaning of the text. But Wilkinson is not content, and so he dives headlong into some amazing statements.

We will start with his least harmful "error" (if there is such a thing), and work our way down. "As God's chosen, blessed sons and daughters, we are expected to attempt something large enough that failure is guaranteed ... unless God steps in (p. 47)." As far as it goes, this statement holds water, but Wilkinson never leaves room for the possibility that we can get in over our heads in ministry and in life. For example, Barnabas was wise enough in Acts 11:19-26 to realize that the ministry at Antioch was too much for him, so he brought Paul to help him. Dependency upon God is a biblical concept, but to recognize that not every believer is equipped to handle every task is biblical as well. Wilkinson does not mention this possibility. More germane to Wilkinson's handling of Scripture is the fact that he cannot draw this concept from I Chronicles 4:9,10. We cannot substantiate that Jabez was launching out into deep waters of dependency on God. We only know that he wants God's hand on him for protection and increased land holdings.

Next the author equates Jabez asking for the hand of God on his life with a Christian being filled with the Holy Spirit; therefore, we should ask to be filled by the Holy Spirit as Jabez and the early church did (see pp. 54-56). First, the Old Testament believers were not normally filled with the Spirit as the New Testament Christians are, so it is quite a stretch to equate the two. Secondly, nowhere, even in the New Testament, did the saints ask to be filled with the Spirit. In Acts 2:42-47, for example, the early Christians did not ask for God's filling; they just lived out their Christian life with enthusiasm and God filled them. The filling of the Spirit comes when we meet the conditions for filling, not when we ask for it.

Most importantly, Wilkinson takes great liberty with the text when he writes, "Notice that Jabez did not begin his prayer by asking for God's hand to be with him. At that point, he didn't sense the need. Things were still manageable. His risks, and the fear that go with them, were minimal. But when his boundaries got moved out, and the kingdom-sized tasks of God's agenda started coming at him, Jabez knew he needed a divine hand—and fast" (pp. 48,49).

Where in the world did Wilkinson get this insight? There is no indication anywhere in the passage that Jabez prayed this prayer more than once, or in sections. Wilkinson **imagines** that Jabez prayed the first two lines—then much later, after God had enlarged his borders and he received "kingdom-sized tasks" (of which nothing is mentioned in the text), he goes back to God and prays line three. This supposition is unwarranted. Peter's warning of the untaught and unstable who distort the Scriptures comes to mind (II Peter 3:16), except we know that Wilkinson is not untaught. He is well trained in the principles of biblical study. What could be his possible reason for twisting the Scriptures in such a manner?

And that You would keep me from evil!

Our first task is to determine what these words mean. The NASB translates them, *"and that Thou wouldest keep me from harm."* That is quite a difference in translation, so let's take a look. The Hebrew word translated *evil* can mean morally evil, distress, bad, or misery. It can range from displeasing to injurious to bad or evil (according to the *Theological Wordbook of the Old Testament*), all depending on the context.

But of course that has been our problem all along in interpreting this passage—we have no context. And because we have no context, the meaning of this phrase can vary from "keep me from committing evil" to "keep evil (or harm) from happening to me." Either would be legitimate, but neither can be definitely determined from our study of the text.

For some inexplicable reason, Wilkinson skips the last line of the Jabez prayer which reads, *"that it may not pain me"* (NASB)! The Hebrew word for *pain* is very similar to the word for *pain* in verse 9. Barnes suggests that he is praying, "Grant that the grief implied in my name may not come upon me!" This would be a proper interpretation in keeping with the literal rendering of the phrase in Hebrew. Uniting this phrase with the one above, we would come away with the best interpretation: that Jabez was praying that God would keep him from injury or harm, most likely at the hands of others. This would be in opposition to Wilkinson's understanding of the passage.

Nevertheless, in true form Wilkinson decides that Jabez was praying that he would not commit evil. He then goes on to develop the subject of praying to be kept from evil. The basic idea of the chapter is not without elements of truth, but it is once again based on eisegesis, not exegesis. He has brought to the text what he wants to teach; he is not explaining what the text teaches. This should seriously disturb all true lovers of the Word of God.

Another issue should be addressed here as well. When Wilkinson states, "Jabez's last request is a brilliant but little-understood **strategy** for sustaining a blessed life" (emphasis mine) (p. 63), he is reducing, once again, the Jabez prayer down to a neat little prescription that will guarantee a blessed life. If we have discovered and learned to use the right combination, we can "release" God's power (pp. 48, 87, 91), we are often told. "You will know beyond doubt that God has opened heaven's storehouses because you prayed" (p. 84). But prayer is not a gimmick to box God into a corner so that He has to give up "the good stuff." In this book on prayer, Wilkinson has repeatedly reduced this glorious privilege to an incantation that supposedly unlocks the blessings we want.

HONORABLE JABEZ

As Wilkinson begins to draw his book to a close, his exegesis does not improve. He tells us that Jabez's "prayer earned him a 'more honorable' award from God" (p. 76). Once again, Wilkinson **is just making up what he wants to say**. Actually the text says that Jabez was more honorable than his brothers (v. 9) before he called on God in this prayer (v. 10). In other words, he was already an honorable man (at least more honorable than his brothers), and his prayer reflected his character. He did not become honorable by praying the "Jabez Prayer." This of course is not the author's thesis (which is that by praying a simple prayer we become honorable and release the power of God to bless us), so it is ignored.

MONEY BACK GUARANTEE?

Like any number of television infomercials, Wilkinson ends his book with a thirty-day challenge: "I challenge you to make the Jabez prayer for blessing part of the daily fabric of your life. To do that, I encourage you to follow unwaveringly the plan outlined here for the next thirty days. By the end of that time, you'll be noticing significant changes in your life, and the prayer will be on its way to becoming a treasured, lifelong habit" (p. 86). He then gives his reader a six-step program (pp. 86-87) to making the **Jabez prayer** a daily habit so that the reader can enjoy the **Jabez blessing** and the **Jabez miracles** being released from heaven.

Of course, with all good advertisement, there must be a disclaimer. So here it comes: "It's only what you believe will happen and therefore do next that will release God's power for you and bring about a life change. But when you act, you will step up to God's best for you" (p. 87).

Throughout the book, Wilkinson has used the same techniques, rhetoric, and methodology that the Word of Faith (prosperity gospel) teachers use:

- God will "exchange your want for His plenty" (p. 17).

- "Your life will be marked by miracles" (p. 25).

- Constant promises of the miraculous and prosperity.

- The power of God being released through the spoken word (prayer) or some other gimmick.

- The disclaimer is that if you fail it is because you do not believe strongly enough—so don't blame us.

- Theology firmly planted in stories and testimony rather than the Word of God.

- The twisting and distorting of Scripture to make it say what the writer wants it to say, rather than what God intended to communicate.

All of these elements are present in *The Prayer of Jabez*. Books like this are never based upon careful exegesis, but on obscure, out-of-context passages bolstered by individual and personal experiences that are supposed to prove the case. In fact, *The Prayer of Jabez* is a thinly disguised version of the prosperity gospel. It is (perhaps unintentionally) designed to deceive those who may detect the folly of many false teachers, but do not have the biblical discernment to recognize the same untruth when it comes from a respected and unsuspected source.

CHAPTER THREE

A PLEA FOR DISCERNMENT

When I first read *The Prayer of Jabez* and heard of the incredible popularity that the book was enjoying, my response was, "Where has all the discernment gone?" Surely the majority of believers would recognize such an obviously flawed approach to Scripture and the Christian life. But it has not been so, and Jabez marches on to conquer new worlds. What has gone wrong? Could it be that the Fundamental/evangelical church is adrift on a sea of subjectivity? Lately she seems to be tossed about by every wind of doctrine (Ephesians 4:14). If a well-known Christian personality develops a new formula for spirituality and backs it with testimonials, the average believer seems all too willing to buy into every line.

Consider what Wilkinson, via Jabez, is teaching:

- That the verbatim repetition of an obscure Old Testament prayer should be at the heart of the prayer life of the Christian.

- That this obscure prayer is to set the pattern for our own prayer life—even though the specific meaning of the prayer is unknown.

- That this obscure prayer, which is never mentioned nor alluded to in the rest of Scripture, is the most important prayer in the Bible.

- That proper exegesis of a passage of Scripture is not important.

- That it is acceptable for a reader of Scripture to force any meaning they desire (eisegesis) upon the text. They are also free to make up their own interpretation, even if such an interpretation is clearly imaginary and/or wishful thinking.

- That it is perfectly proper to apply any passage of Scripture to our own lives, even if that application is based upon a faulty interpretation.

- That the ultimate proof of truth is not the correct understanding of Scripture, but anecdotal testimony (i.e., experience).

- That a prayer, any prayer, guarantees release of God's favor and miraculous power.

- That "selfish praying delights the heart of God."

- That the "blessed" life can be reduced to a formula, a gimmick, or a strategy (p. 63).

When Christians can be so easily deceived, biblical perception is obviously lacking. Fed for too long on nothing but the milk of the Word, and persuaded by leaders to believe that this diet is sound, few Christians are going on to maturity in Christ (Hebrews 5:11-14). Having never been taught the simplest methods of Bible study, they are unable to recognize when the Scriptures are being distorted. The result is that they are easy prey for all sorts of unintentional and intentional deceptions that are constantly bombarding the church. My plea is that an increasing number of believers will drop their hot pursuit for Christianity "Lite" and take up the serious study of the Word of God.

Our evaluation of *The Prayer of Jabez* has been as much a concern for the state of discernment in the conservative church as it has been a criticism of Wilkinson's little book. As the church rides the wave of the market-driven church strategy, she often feels secure in her success. People are coming to services in droves, churches are growing, and new buildings are popping up all over suburbia. But I fear this apparent success is a mile wide and an inch deep, for when these folks gather in services, they are too often not being taught either the Word of God or how to personally understand the Scriptures. The results are shallow Christians, easily deceived by any new gimmick or fad that merges into their pathway. And deceived

Christians do not live out the life God intended for them. Paul told the Colossians that his aim was to present every man complete in Christ (Colossians 1:28). He did that by teaching the whole counsel of God (Acts 20:27). Sentimental music and peppy stories may draw crowds, but mature believers are not developed by such methodology. A return to solid, well-exegeted Bible teaching, based on normal/literal hermeneutics, is imperative if the tide is to be turned in this great battle.

What the church is experiencing today, I believe, is the beginning of the fallout that inevitably accompanies an abandonment of truth. In order to become successful, the church-growth gurus have convinced us that we must go easy on truth and heavy on things the consumer desires, such as self-fulfillment, entertainment, and prosperity. Yet God's church is to be *the pillar and support of the truth* (I Timothy 3:15), not the place where people are told what they want to hear. The conservative church is becoming increasingly hollowed out as it exchanges its biblical purpose for one that is market-suggested. Many local congregations still have the outward shell that allows them to resemble Christ's church, but the substance is gone, and in time they will collapse spiritually.

Our plea is a return to the Scriptures, and an abandonment of story-theology. We must reject the fluff that masquerades as Bible teaching. We must read and study the Bible as it was meant to be encountered, refusing to be taken in by testimonials and success stories that do not emerge clearly from the Word of God. This is the true aim behind our study of Jabez. It is not enough to expose the specific errors of one book, for another will soon rise to take its place. No, the need is for biblical discernment that comes only through a solid working knowledge of the precious Word of God.

CHAPTER FOUR

AN OVERVIEW OF HERMENEUTICAL PRINCIPLES

Hermeneutics is the science and art that teaches the principles, laws, and methods of interpretation. Although often ignored, it is commonly accepted in Fundamental/evangelical circles that the only proper hermeneutic for the interpretation of Scripture is the normal/literal approach. All other hermeneutics will lead us astray in the true understanding of the biblical text. This would be a good time to share some of the key principles found within the normal/literal approach to Scripture:

1. We work from the assumption that the Bible is authoritative. The Bible itself is not a normal book; it is the unique and only authoritative Word of God to mankind today, but God gave it in a way that allows us to use a normal/literal method of interpreting it.

2. The Bible interprets itself; Scripture best explains Scripture.

3. Scripture never contradicts Scripture. There may be apparent discrepancies, but these are only apparent. When all texts are properly interpreted, they will be in harmony.

4. Interpret personal experience in light of Scripture, and not Scripture in light of personal experience. (Many of the concepts found in *The Prayer of Jabez* are derived from personal testimony, not drawn from Scripture.)

5. Biblical examples are authoritative only when supported by a command. Just because God caused, allowed, or promised a certain thing to an individual or nation in the Bible, does not mean that He will do the same thing in

our lives. (Ignoring this principle is a common error in many Christian writings, and is at the heart of the misguided teaching found in *The Prayer of Jabez.)*

6. A given passage of Scripture has only one meaning, not several, unless the Word of God clearly indicates otherwise. The job of the Bible student is to discover that one meaning, not make up what he wants the passage to say. (Wilkinson is guilty of violating this principle as well.)

7. Interpret a passage in harmony with its context. Few principles of Bible interpretation are as important as this one, and few are so frequently ignored. (Had Wilkinson interpreted I Chronicles 4:9,10 in context, he would not have written his book.)

A number of inadequate hermeneutical approaches have been developed over the years. The best known of these faulty hermeneutics are:

• The allegorical approach, which attempts to find concealed, secret, or symbolic meaning behind simple words, narratives, and stories. To the disciple of this method, the real intent of a passage is to be found in the hidden meaning, not in the actual words or account.

• The devotional approach is a moderate form of the allegorical. Under this methodology, the Bible student accepts the normal/literal meaning of the text, but then also searches for a devotional or spiritualized understanding. That Orpah kissed Naomi and then departed, but Ruth clung to Naomi and stayed is a literal fact (Ruth 1:14). The devotional approach will also add a spiritual meaning behind these words: Ruth was devoted to Naomi, as the Christian should be devoted to Christ. She not only gives lip service, but clings to her Lord. While this concept is true biblically, it is not the meaning of Ruth 1:4. Something has been read into this passage that was never intended in this text of Scripture. This is a well-meaning but seriously dangerous approach to Scripture.

• The liberal approach is to reinterpret any and all Scriptures that offend the modern mind. If a normal/literal understanding of a passage is not in line with the teaching of science, it must be jettisoned. If certain teachings of the epistles are not politically correct, they must be explained as part of another culture and not applicable for today.

• The neo-orthodox approach teaches that the Bible, or anything else for that matter, **becomes** the Word of God when God uses it to speak to us in a specific manner. The Scriptures are not God's unique revelation to man until God chooses to use it to impress His word on our hearts.

Bruce Wilkinson, being a graduate of Dallas Theological Seminary, would surely proclaim that he both understands and believes in the commonly accepted principles of the normal/literal hermeneutic. In practice, however, for reasons that are quite inexplicable, he has chosen to ignore these principles and write a book using the devotional methodology. The result is that Wilkinson has elevated a little-known, and seemingly unimportant, prayer to be the very apex of the Christian life and experience. (Compare this prayer to some of David's or Paul's or Jesus', especially John 17, and ask yourself, "Why has the author chosen the prayer of Jabez?") Unfortunately, as we have shown, *The Prayer of Jabez* is not a proper interpretation of I Chronicles 4:9,10 at all. Rather, the author has chosen to spiritualize the text. He made up what he wants it to mean, called for an application based upon his faulty exegesis, underwrote the whole thing with testimonies and anecdotes instead of Scripture, and foisted it upon the church as the long-lost key that will unlock the unfathomable blessings of God.

Nothing could be more absurd—unless, of course, a massive number of God's people are deceived by such a fad. And, sadly, this is what has happened.

SECTION TWO

HOW TO STUDY THE BIBLE

INTRODUCTION

Since the real issue on the table with regard to *The Prayer of Jabez* is the use and misuse of Scripture, I thought it wise to include a short manual on how to study the Bible. This manual is designed especially to be used by small group Bible studies, although it could be profitably used by an individual student. To provide a user-friendly format that will be effective as a teaching tool, some duplication of Chapter Four will be noted.

LESSON ONE

BIBLE READING AND HERMENEUTICS

INTRODUCTION

1. **Why do people find it so hard to study the Bible?** (Should be used as an opening discussion question.)

While all Christians proclaim the importance of Scripture, relatively few read or study the Bible on a consistent basis. It is the goal of this study to eliminate as many barriers as possible.

2. Why should Christians study the Bible?

Howard Hendricks, in *Living by the Book*, gives three important reasons:
> a. It is essential to spiritual growth (I Pet. 2:2).
> b. It is essential to spiritual maturity (Heb. 5:11-14).
> c. It is essential to spiritual effectiveness (II Tim. 3:16-17).

SCRIPTURE DOES NOT YIELD ITS FRUIT TO THE LAZY.

I. BIBLE READING

We should be readers of the Bible before we attempt to be students of the Bible. Some helpful suggestions:

1. It will take discipline. Make Bible reading and study a priority.

2. You should have a definite time to read each day (e.g., 8 a.m. or during lunch break).

3. Begin by scheduling 5-15 minutes a day for Bible reading. Do not attempt to start

out by pledging an hour for daily Bible study. You may not be able to keep up the pace and will soon give up.

4. You should have a definite place to read each day. Find a quiet spot away from people and distractions. Keep your Bible, notebook, study aids, and pens or pencils in a convenient location so that they are handy.

5. Be realistic in your expectations. Don't expect bells and whistles every time you read your Bible. The goal of Bible study is not to give you goosebumps, but to equip you to live for Christ.

6. Be consistent and persevere. By reading only one chapter a day, you will read through the Bible in a little over three years. (You can read through the Bible in one year by reading three chapters per day and five on Sunday.)

7. Vary your readings. Alternate between Old and New Testament books. Alternate between different types of literature. For example, after reading the narrative

accounts of the Gospels or Genesis, read doctrinal sections such as the epistles. After reading heavy prophecy such as Isaiah, you may want to move to worship portions like Psalms or practical books like Proverbs. One year you may try to read through the whole Bible, and the next you may want to read four epistles over and over until you have mastered their content.

8. Select a good Bible translation. Three types of translations are:

- **PARAPHRASE:** examples include *The Living Bible* (or *Living Bible Translation*), *Phillips*, and *The Message*. These are not translations as such, but paraphrases that give the general idea of the original. Paraphrases are not suitable for Bible study and have limited value for Bible reading.

- **LITERAL:** Examples include the *King James Bible*, *The New King James Bible*, and *The New American Standard Bible*. All three of these are faithful translations from the original Greek and Hebrew. They attempt to be as literal as possible. These are the best for study.

- **DYNAMIC EQUIVALENT:** The best example is the *New International Version*, which is the fastest selling translation today. The *NIV* is a hybrid between paraphrase and literal. It is a translation that takes considerable liberties compared to the literal translation, seeking to translate the thought rather than the actual words. All translations involve some interpretation, but with the *NIV*, far too much is interpreted rather than translated. The *NIV* is easy reading, but has limited value for serious study. A clear difference among the types of translations can be seen by reading Romans 8:5, 8-9 from all three types. Note that the Greek is well represented by the NASB, which translates *sarkos* as "flesh." The passage is speaking of unbelievers, who are in the flesh, as opposed to believers who are in the Spirit. The literal translation of verse 9 is that we believers "are not in the flesh." Note how the NIV changes the whole meaning of the text by translating it, "You are not controlled by your sinful nature but by the Spirit." This translation gives the impression that Paul is giving believers options concerning what will control their lives (the flesh or the Spirit). That is an important issue, but not the subject matter of Romans 8. The NIV has translated the Greek preposition *en* (meaning "in") as "controlled by" and *sarkos* (meaning "flesh") as "sinful nature." This is interpretation, not translation.

9. *Just a word about study Bibles:* Study Bibles are not translations; rather, study Bibles take one of the standard translations and add a particular set of notes that reflect certain views or doctrinal positions. Some of the best (although we would not endorse all the notes from any) include: The *Scofield Reference Bible,* the *Ryrie Study Bible,* and the *MacArthur Study Bible.* Caution is needed here. First, it has become increasingly popular to publish study Bibles that reflect a multitude of positions. Hundreds of study Bibles are on the market today, many of which have added very unfortunate and often inaccurate notes. Next, do not let study Bibles study the Bible for you. Even the best can be a trap if you let them do your thinking for you. Their notes should supplement your own personal study.

10. Read slowly and carefully. Never speed-read the Bible. Reading aloud often aids in concentration. Keep in mind that these are the very words of God.

11. Take notes in a notebook, Bible, or both.

II. Hermeneutics:

1. **Definition:** The science that teaches the principles, laws, and methods of interpretation.

2. The vast majority of theological errors and doctrinal disagreements are rooted in different approaches to hermeneutics (or ways of interpreting the Bible). It is not so much what the Bible says that causes differences of opinion—it is how we approach what the Bible says.

3. Some of the best-known schools of hermeneutics are:

   • **ALLEGORICAL:** An attempt to find and read into Scripture hidden, secondary meaning rather than reading the plain words of the text.

- **DEVOTIONAL:** Adding a devotional flavor to the normal interpretation. This is a mild form of allegorical interpretation, and a misguided attempt at application.

- **LIBERAL:** Whatever is not in harmony with the educated mentality (what is scientific or politically correct at the time) is to be rejected.

- **NEO-ORTHODOX:** The Scriptures are not the Word of God, but contain the Word of God. In other words, whatever inspires you is the Word of God to you. This could include a song, a novel, or a newspaper. The Bible becomes the Word of God to you when it inspires you. This is very different from the belief that the inspired words of God are contained only in Scripture.

- **NORMAL (LITERAL):** Also known as the Grammatical-Historical approach in which Scripture is read normally (just as other literature is). It presupposes that God has given His revelation in an intelligent and understandable form. It further presupposes that the Bible is understandable through common sense and the application of the normal rules of grammar and history, as aided by the Holy Spirit.

4. Some simple rules or assumptions that guide our interpretation of Scripture:

  • Scripture can be understood.

  • Scripture contains all the truth we need for godly living (II Tim. 3:16, 17).

  • Scripture interprets Scripture (therefore, clear passages should interpret obscure passages).

  • Scripture never contradicts itself. There may be apparent discrepancies, but these are only apparent. When all texts are properly interpreted, they will be in harmony.

  • Scripture has only one meaning in a given passage. ("What it means to me" is not the correct question;

"What God meant to say" is.)

- Scripture must be interpreted in context. (Taking Scripture out of context results in a multitude of interpretation errors. Therefore, we will spend additional time on context in future lessons.)

- Scripture is authoritative. It is the final word on all it addresses.

- Scripture's purpose is to change lives, not just fill heads.

CONCLUSION

1. We will be following a three-step approach on how to study the Bible: observation, interpretation, and application. Let's make some observations in the book of I John. (Give students time to make observations on the first four verses of I John. Share a few of these observations with the class. If time, have them finish chapter one. Do not allow them to interpret what they have observed. Help them to see a clear distinction between observation and interpretation.)

2. ***Homework****:* Read I John three times this week:

- First time: read through at one sitting with no markings.

- Second time: read through and mark recurring words.

- Third time: read through jotting down any observations that interest you. Bring these with you next time.

LESSON TWO

OBSERVATIONS

OBSERVATION

Go over the homework assignment from last session. Make certain that you do this every week; otherwise, you will discover students showing up without their homework (the old "dog ate my homework" ploy).

Bible Study involves three steps: *Observation* (what do I see); *Interpretation* (what does it mean); and *Application* (how do I make this a reality in my life?).

Observation involves reading, recording, and reflecting. As we read, we should record our observations. Look for important themes, words, doctrines, people, etc. It is not desirable to attempt to solve all problems and deal with all issues at this point. It is important to record a number of observations and spend a little time reflecting upon them.

In-class project*:* Take three minutes and record all the observations that you can on Revelation 2:1-7. (After exactly three minutes, have the class make observations. Allow for volunteers. If no one speaks up, call on people who would not be embarrassed.)

NINE STRATEGIES TO FIRST-RATE OBSERVATIONS

(Some of these strategies are taken from *Living by the Book* by Howard Hendricks.)

READ THOUGHTFULLY

Don't throw your mind into neutral. Apply the same mental discipline that you would to any subject in which you take a vital interest (finances, cars, decorating, sports).

Record your thoughts in your Bible or notebook.

In-class project*:* Read III John. (Have the text read out loud, then ask the questions, allowing the students to give answers.) Barrage the text with questions. What do we know about the situation or occasion for the letter? What feelings are evident? What issues are being dealt with?

Do we have any similar issues today? What questions remain unanswered (i.e., what is it that we do not know)?

READ REPEATEDLY

Read the same passage (e.g., a small book or section of a larger book) several times over the course of a few weeks. For example, read Colossians once per day for two weeks, or read John 1–7 (one third of the Gospel of John) five times, then move on to John 8–14, doing the same. Finally, read John 15–21 using the same approach.

READ PATIENTLY

The fruit of the Word takes time to ripen, and many get disillusioned with the process. This is especially true if someone is looking for entertainment rather than enlightenment.

By reading one book per month, a person will study through the Bible in 5½ years.

READ SELECTIVELY

Six questions to ask any passage of Scripture: *who, what, where, when, why,* and *wherefore* (so what? what difference does it make?).

In-class project: Try this on Psalm 52. (Have the students read the Psalm silently and then ask them the questions.)

READ PRAYERFULLY

We should ask God for wisdom and insight as we read the text of Scripture.

READ DIVERSELY

Vary your readings: Use different translations; read from different portions of Scripture; develop projects.

READ MEDITATIVELY

Learn to reflect on Scripture. Don't be in a hurry. "We can't be holy in a hurry."

READ PURPOSEFULLY

Look for the intent of the author. Why has he written this particular book? What is its purpose?

In-class project: Examine the following: John 20:30, 31; Deuteronomy 1:1; Proverbs 1:1-6; Luke 1:1-4; I John 5:13. What were the author's purposes in writing these books according to the passages above?

READ CONTEXTUALLY

This means viewing the parts in light of the whole, especially its stated purpose (if it has one). Pay attention to the context.

Homework: Complete word study chart by noting where each of the listed words is found in I John. (This chart is an expanded version of a similar one found in the *Inductive Study Bible*.)

1 JOHN KEY WORDS

Chapter	Fellowship	Abide	Sin	Know	Love	Born of God	Write	Light
1								
2								
3								
4								
5								
Total								

Chapter	Truth	Life	World	Witness	Liar	Commandments	Believe	Children
1								
2								
3								
4								
5								
Total								

LESSON THREE

INTERPRETATION

INTERPRETATION

Once solid observations have been made, we are ready to begin the next step: interpretation. There are a number of difficulties that confront the Bible student at this point, including language and cultural issues. In order to understand a scriptural passage correctly these difficulties must be overcome.

To interpret Scripture accurately, we must keep a number of things in mind, including the importance of the "Big Picture." Once the observation stage is complete, we should have a good idea of the direction the author is going. The next step is to take a careful look at the big picture by studying the paragraphs involved in our text.

Working with a paragraph. (Helps on how to find a paragraph in the Bible: The NIV is written in paragraph form. The NASB has bold print at the verse number in which a new paragraph begins. Paragraphs are not inspired and so are only suggestions by the translators, but are certainly worth considering.)

1. ***In-class project:*** Using Philippians 4:1-9, notice how the subject changes at the paragraph breaks. The paragraphs are connected, but contain separate thoughts. Look for anything that is emphasized. Emphasis can be found by noting how much space is given to a given subject, or by repetition of words, terms, concepts, etc.

2. ***In-class project:*** Find the repetition in the following passages: Psalm 119; II Corinthians 1:3-7, 2:1-7. What subject is the author addressing in each passage?

3. ***In-class project:*** Look for things that are related or similar, metaphors, and word pictures. What can be found in John 15:1-10; John 3:3-7?

4. Look for connecting words such as "but" and "therefore." What does the "therefore" in Romans 12:1 tell us?

5. Look for the big picture before you try to analyze the details.

ALWAYS KEEP THE CONTEXT IN MIND

Most errors of interpretation are made by taking passages out of context. By applying the principles found under the previous section, most errors can be avoided.

Circles of context

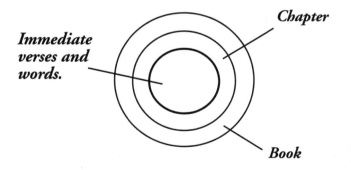

Immediate verses and words.

Chapter

Book

In-class project: Read together Matthew 18:20. What does it seem to mean? Now read the context (18:15-20). What does this verse mean in context?

REMEMBER THAT SCRIPTURE NEVER CONTRADICTS SCRIPTURE

Since Scripture never contradicts itself, it is important that we compare Scripture with Scripture when searching for the meaning of a text, especially a difficult one.

In-class project: Compare Galatians 3:28 with I Timothy 2:11, 12. Do these two passages conflict? What does Scripture teach about women in relationship to the church according to these two passages?

TAKE CAREFUL NOTE TO WHOM A PASSAGE OF SCRIPTURE IS WRITTEN

Different cultures and dispensations must be kept in mind as we study the Word. Also, the intended audience must be noticed. Some Scripture is addressed to a specific person(s) or nation, and cannot be applied directly to us.

In-class project: Read Jeremiah 29:11. To whom is this verse addressed? Can any of this verse be applied to us? Can all of it? Compare Jeremiah 31:38, 32:42, and Lamentations 3:38.

MAKE WISE USE OF STUDY TOOLS

This is the use of secondary resources: concordances, Bible dictionaries and handbooks, atlases, and commentaries. Secondary resources are excellent tools in the understanding of Scripture, but should be used only after personal study. (We will look at this issue more closely in Lesson #6.)

PRINCIPLES FOR FIGURING OUT THE FIGURATIVE

Figurative language in Scripture can be problematic. The following are some principles, taken from Hendricks, pp. 257-267, which can be very useful when faced with the figurative:

1. Use the literal unless there is some good reason not to. For example: Luke 13:32 calls Herod a fox; actually he was a man who behaved like a fox. While the Song of Solomon is to be taken literally, note obvious figurative language that is not to be understood literally (e.g., 2:8, 9).

2. Use the figurative sense when the passage tells you to do so. For example: the dreams of Joseph are said to be symbolic (Genesis 41:25-32).

3. Use the figurative if a literal meaning is impossible, immoral, or absurd. For example: see John 6:53-55. Not understanding

this principle, many misunderstood Jesus (see v. 60).

4. Use the figurative sense if the expression is an obvious figure of speech. See Proverbs 11:22; I Corinthians 15:55; Psalm 63:7.

5. Use the figurative sense if a literal interpretation goes contrary to the plan and purpose of the author, or is contrary to the rest of Scripture (remember Scripture interprets Scripture). For example: Psalm 1:3 appears to, but does not, guarantee material prosperity. How do we know this? Compare Hebrews 11:36-38.

Homework: Write down everything that the epistle of I John tells us we can know:

LESSON FOUR

APPLICATION

APPLICATION
The purpose of application is to make Bible knowledge relevant to us personally, so that our lives are pleasing to God. Howard Hendriksen is on the money when he says, "The Bible was not written to satisfy our curiosity. It was written to transform our lives" (James 1:23-25). Everyone wants the blessing of God, but not everyone is responding to the revelation of God. Someone said, "Many Christians are like poor photographs: overexposed and underdeveloped."

THE APPLICATION PROCESS
1. Understand the Passage
Knowing what the text is saying should have

been achieved during the observation stage. Knowing what the text means is the purpose of the interpretation stage. Application should only be attempted after we have completed these two steps and are confident that we understand what the passage is teaching. Keep in mind that there is only one meaning for any given text.

2. The "So What" Question

It is at this point that we ask, "So what?" That is, "Now that I know what the passage is teaching, how does it (or should it) affect my life?" While there is only one meaning for any given text, there may be numerous applications.

There are two types of applications: general and specific. General applications are those that could (or should) be true for anyone examining a particular passage. Specific applications are applications that are unique to you.

For example: Romans 12:19a tells us to "never take our own revenge, but leave room for the wrath of God."

• The meaning of this verse is clear: rather than seeking revenge when someone wrongs us, we need to leave the situation in the hands of God.

• A general application might be that we should not get angry and seek revenge against our neighbors who may occasionally irritate us. Anyone who has neighbors could make this application.

• A specific application might be that you would not seek revenge against Joe Smith, who often lets his dog, Porky, "explore" in your yard, leaving interesting evidence that he has been there.

In-class project*:* What is the meaning of Philippians 4:6? What are some general applications? What is your specific application? For example: What is it that you tend to worry about, and how does this passage apply?

3. Reflection

Spend time thinking about the passage of Scripture under study and how it applies to your life. One of the best ways to do this is in prayer.

Reflection is not contemplation of some abstract truth; it is a practical consideration of how to put the truth of God's Word to work in our lives. It is during reflection that we can do three things:

• Define our objective by making it specific and obtainable. Don't say, "I am not going to get angry any more." Instead say, "My goal is to not blow up at Joe for allowing Porky to hide presents in my yard."

• Come up with a plan. The next time Joe and Porky visit, how are you going to handle the situation so that you do not get angry, but yet you express clearly that Porky's visits are unwanted?

• Follow through: Put your plan into action. See "practice" below.

4. Make Changes

Put into practice the application(s) that you have made. It is not until this step has been taken that true application has taken place. Go over the whole process by using the following three-column sheet and studying the word "world" as used in I John. Find all the places in I John where the word "world" is found. Write down any observations. Next, go back through and interpret the meaning of "world" in this epistle. Note that you will find more than one meaning, depending on the context and word usage. Finally, make general applications for the world as found in I John 2:15-17:

OBSERVATION	INTERPRETATION	APPLICATION

Homework: Read the book of Titus several times this week. Using the three-column application sheet, make observations of the book.

PASSAGE BEING STUDIED:

OBSERVATION	INTERPRETATION	APPLICATION

LESSON FIVE

THE SURVEY
METHOD, PART 1

For those who desire to dig a little deeper, the survey method of Bible study is very helpful. This method will require more effort, but will yield wonderful fruit. While learning this method, we recommend using a short epistle such as II Peter, Colossians, or Philippians. For our study together, we will use Titus.

THE SURVEY METHOD:
Historical background

It is very helpful in Bible study to know the historical background of the passage you wish to study. Understanding who the author is, to whom he is writing, the time frame, and so forth, will greatly aid in your comprehension of the text under study. Such information is easily obtained in the introductory sections of any good study Bible. For more detailed information, consult a Bible dictionary, handbook, or a good commentary.

Order

1. Choose a book of the Bible and begin to survey it by reading it through a number of times. This is the same step as observation in our previous studies.

2. Begin to analyze the book by breaking it into sections, most likely according to paragraphs.

3. Go back and write a short description of (or give a title to) each paragraph.

4. Based on your observations and descriptions, discover and write out the theme of the book. You are looking for the general subject of the epistle.

5. Go back through the epistle and observe how each paragraph relates to the theme.

At this point, you might develop a rough outline of the book.

6. Next, analyze each section more carefully. Were your observations, interpretations, and descriptions correct? If not, make adjustments.

7. Now you can complete your outline, developing it according to the theme of the book.

8. The ambitious might even create a chart showing the theme of the book and its outline.

9. If more study is desired, begin to examine each verse within the paragraphs, and even individual words.

The survey method using Titus

1. Using Bible study tools (see Lesson #6), find out what the historical background and setting are for the book of Titus. Find Corinth and Crete on the maps found in your Bible. Don't allow yourself to be tempted to look at the outlines and analysis that can be found in these tools. Don't

lose the joy of firsthand discovery of biblical truth.

2. Next, share the observations that were made from Titus (the homework assignment for this week).

3. Identify the paragraphs, using the NASB.

4. After reading each paragraph, decide what the subject of that paragraph is. Use the preliminary study chart to record your findings.

PRELIMINARY STUDY OF TITUS

SUBJECT	TITLE
1:1-4	
1:5-9	
1:10-16	
2:1-10	
2:11-15	
3:1-11	
3:12-15	

Theme:

Homework: Going back over the book of Titus, re-examine the subjects of each paragraph. From this study, decide on a theme for Titus. Next, go back and develop a title for each paragraph that is related to the theme.

Lesson Six

The Survey Method, Part 2

The survey method concluded

1. From your homework assignment, share some possible themes for Titus. Why have you chosen this particular theme?

2. As a class, take two or three of the possible themes offered, and give titles to the paragraphs that would fit well with the themes.

3. As a class, create an outline for Titus, making use of one of the themes and corresponding titles.

4. Make a chart for Titus using one of the themes and corresponding titles (see chart on page 106).

5. At this point, and not until this point, you should have a good understanding of the context and are ready for deeper study, if desired.

BIBLE STUDY TOOLS

A number of Bible study tools can be very helpful in your understanding of the Scriptures. The following are a few of the best:

• *Vine's Expository Dictionary:* allows you to look up an English word and find its Hebrew or Greek counterpart and the meaning of the word.

• Bible dictionaries: are excellent for discovering information about biblical names, places, events, customs, etc.

• Concordances: enable you to find an English word in the Scriptures. For example: Look up "love" and you will find the location of every time the word "love" is used in the Bible.

Some concordances (such as *Young's* and *Strong's*) also offer limited help in understanding the meaning of words.

• Computer programs such as the *Online Bible* serve as a combination of a concordance and *Vines*, among other things. One advantage of using computer programs is that you can look up phrases as well as words.

• *Unger's Bible Handbook:* source of overview, information, and general commentary.

• *Nave's Topical Bible*: indexes the Bible according to topic. For example: Look up the subject of "gluttony" and find all Scriptures that deal with that issue.

• Commentaries: Commentaries on every book in the Bible are available. *The Bible Knowledge Commentary* (two volumes) would be a great choice for a commentary covering the whole Bible. Keep in mind that commentaries are not inspired and may be occasionally in error. Nevertheless, good commentaries are of great value.

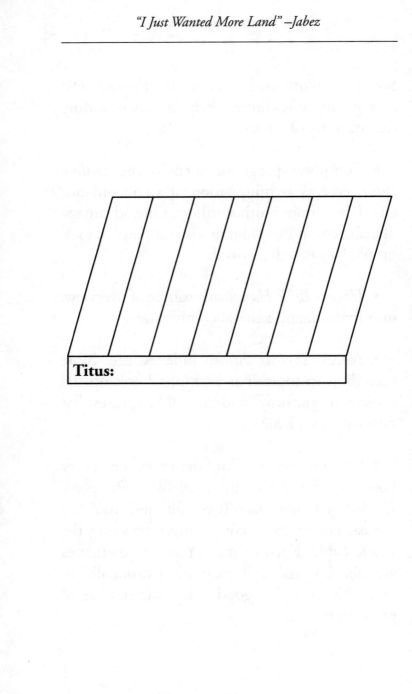

BIOGRAPHY

GARY E. GILLEY is Pastor-teacher at Southern View Chapel in Springfield, Illinois, where he has ministered since 1975. He is also the author of "Think on These Things," a widely circulated monthly publication dealing with contemporary theological issues.

For more information on "Think on These Things" ministries, visit www.svchapel.org.